top 10

recipes for the beginner home cook

top 10

recipes for the beginner home cook

10 simple classic recipes
Learn these and you can cook

This is a book for those who appreciate good food, but have no idea how to prepare it themselves.

If you want to cook to survive yourself or occasionally cook for friends, this book will give you confidence and ideas.

There are ten basic recipes for a range of foods: eggs, soups, pasta, rice, chicken, beef, fish, vegetables, green salad and sorbet.

Once you become confident, there are simple variations on the basic dishes. Your creativity can take you as far as you want.

You will learn what implements you will need, how they work, what various herbs look like and how to stock your cupboard.

When you can cook these 'Top 10' you can call yourself a cook.

* It is **NOT** a guide to 'cheap eating'.

* It is **NOT** a children's cookbook.

* It is **NOT** an 'open a can of beans and pour over sausage' collection of recipes.

* It **IS** about eating delicious, healthy food, simply prepared.

* It **WILL** teach you the simple keys to cooking.

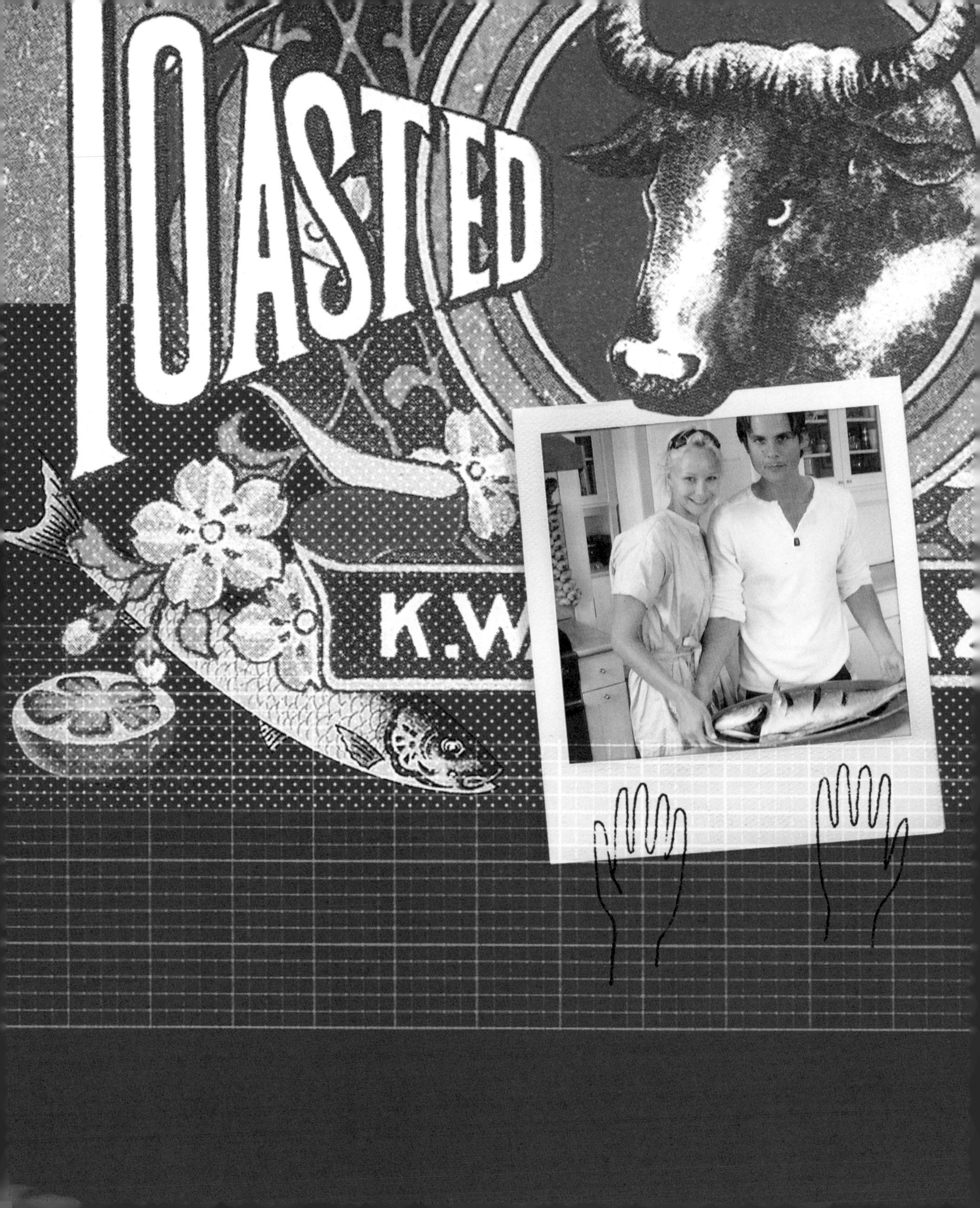
TOASTED
K.W

top 10

If you can cook these, you can cook!

1. eggs

2. soup

3. pasta

4. rice

5. chicken

6. beef

7. fish

8. vegetables

9. green salad

10. sorbet

top 10

1. egg

omelette

The omelette is a classical French dish that transforms eggs into something both elegant and delicious. Ideal for lunch or a light supper, it is very versatile and can be made with all sorts of fillings. Lying plump and golden on a plate, the juices slightly running out, it is simply irresistible.

2. soup

cauliflower soup

One hearty soup should be in everyone's repertoire. Cauliflower is rather unusual and a great favourite of mine. You can use other vegetables to make different soups in much the same way.

3. pasta

pasta with tomato sauce

Everyone loves pasta and it is an 'absolute must' recipe! It is a very quick and simple dish, and can be made rustic or refined by changing the type of pasta. You can use different sauces to create a different dish every time.

4. rice

risotto

Risotto is a dish that should be cooked at home. It never tastes quite as good in a restaurant, because they usually partially precook it. It is not difficult to make, but does take a little time and attention. The result, however, is sublime. It should become your 'signature' dish!

5. chicken

whole chicken roasted in its juices

This is the simplest way to prepare a whole chicken. By baking it in an oven bag, it cooks in its own juices and the flesh remains incredibly moist. The extra bonus: the washing up is minimal!

top 10

6. beef

roasted beef with spicy sauce

This dish is fit for a king. The sauce is rich and unusual and extremely simple to prepare. It is also a dish that tastes delicious cold the next day.

7. fish

whole baked fish

A whole fish looks marvellous and, I think, tastes better than fillets because it cooks in its own juices. The paper bag variation here is culinary theatre at its best when you open it in front of your guests. Choose a very fresh fish!

8. vegetables

roasted mixed vegetables

Transform vegetables into a dish that looks superb and generous, and tastes exceptional. The flavour changes according to season.

9. green salad

mixed salad with a classic dressing

Learn this classic dressing and then choose the leaves for your salad. Fresh leaves and homemade dressing take a simple salad to new heights.

10. sorbet

raspberry sorbet and ice-cream

This is an extremely quick and simple dessert with a spectacular colour! Once you have tasted it you will understand why it is worth making your own rather than buying it.

top 10 *essential herbs*

basil
Great for tomato salads and tomato sauces. Add towards the end of cooking as it loses its flavour easily and turns black.

oregano
Use fresh or dried. Stronger in flavour, great for sauces, meats and vegetables.

parsley
I prefer the Italian flat variety to the curly one. You can use it in any dish you like: soups, omelettes, sauces, vegetables. It can be cooked, or just chopped and sprinkled to finish a dish.

sage
Ideal for veal dishes, in stews, in sauces, or fried in butter until crisp then served on pasta or rice.

rosemary
Great for chicken, beef, or lamb and with roasted vegetables. Can be left whole, then removed after cooking is completed, or chopped finely.

thyme
There are different varieties of thyme, so smell them and see which one you like best. It is ideal for fish, in stews and roasts. It is quite strong in flavour, so you should use it sparingly.

dill
It has an aniseed flavour. It tastes really nice in cucumber salads, on smoked salmon and other fish and in some soups.

chives
The flavour is oniony. It is great in salads or as garnish in some soups. You do not cook it.

bay leaves
Used to flavour sauces, stews, fish and vegetables. You never eat the bay leaf; always discard it after cooking is finished. It is very hard in texture.

coriander
It looks very much like Italian parsley, so always smell it to make sure it is coriander. It is used a lot in Asian dishes. The flavour is quite strong and distinctive.

top 10 *kitchen implements*

mixing bowl

frying pan

spatula

serrated chopping knife

very sharp carving knife

big saucepan

colander

small saucepan

cheese grater

tin opener

wooden spoons

chopping board

roasting tin

garlic crusher

potato peeler

measuring cup

cast iron grill

kitchen wiz

egg

omelette

4 PEOPLE

8 organic eggs.	• Use 2 eggs per person. • Lightly beat eggs in a bowl.
1 teaspoon salt. ground pepper. 1 tablespoon water. ½ cup freshly grated parmigiano.	• Add these to the eggs and mix well.
20 g unsalted butter.	• Melt the butter in a non-stick fry pan. When the butter bubbles lightly, lower the heat and add the egg mixture. • Let it cook a few minutes. • When you see that the eggs are starting to become firm on the side of the pan, gently push the edge of the egg mixture towards the middle of the pan, using a spatula. • Start tipping the pan gently, so that the liquid egg will run into the just created space. • Repeat this until all the liquid egg mixture is used up. • The omelette should still be moist in the middle. Slide half of the omelette on a serving dish and fold it in half.

kitchen implements

omelette

VARIATIONS Before folding the omelette in half, you can add:

1 Chopped fresh herbs such as Italian parsley, oregano or chives.
2 Ham, a couple of slices cut into pieces.
3 Tinned tuna, a small tin of tuna, drained of oil and broken up into pieces.
4 Spinach, 1–2 handfuls of fresh spinach leaves.
5 Salmon, 2–3 slices, cut into strips.
6 Mushrooms. You can cook them in a little butter and garlic and then add them to the omelette.

Did you know that the shell of the egg only hardens once it comes out of the chicken's bum and comes in contact with air? The older the chook, the bigger the egg can get.

shopping list

organic eggs
parmigiano cheese
unsalted butter

Plus any other topping of your choice that you want to add to your omelette.

shaving some parmigiano

notes

soup

cauliflower soup

6 PEOPLE

If you have fresh chicken stock, terrific. If not, use a good quality chicken or vegetable stock cube.

1 firm whole cauliflower.	• Cut into small chunks.
50 g unsalted butter. 2–3 tablespoons virgin olive oil.	• Melt the butter and oil in a large saucepan.
2 leeks.	• Slice them and cook them in the butter and olive oil over a gentle heat for about 5 minutes. They will become slightly transparent and sweet. • Now add the cauliflower pieces and stir them around.
1 glass of dry white wine (optional).	• Add it to the pan and, stirring, let the wine evaporate.

2 litres fresh
  chicken stock or
  2 litres water
  plus 3–4 stock cubes.
	• Add the liquid to the pan, stir, then put the lid on and,
	over a gentle heat, let it cook for about 15–20 minutes.
	• With your kitchen wiz, purée the cauliflower in the pan
	itself. Taste and add salt and pepper to taste.

½ cup cream. ½ cup freshly grated parmigiano.	• Add these to the soup, mix well and take off the heat.
Italian parsley or chives, chopped.	• Sprinkle on top of soup and serve.

kitchen implements

cauliflower soup

VARIATIONS For pumpkin soup:

Use a butternut pumpkin, peel and cut it into small pieces discarding the seeds.
Then proceed as per the cauliflower soup recipe. You will NOT use the wine.
You will NOT use the parmigiano. Instead of chives you can use fresh basil.

pumpkin soup

shopping list

1 firm cauliflower
or butternut pumpkin.

2 leeks

unsalted butter

parmigiano cheese
*not if you're making
pumpkin soup.*

300 ml cream

Italian parsley or chives
basil for pumpkin soup.

virgin olive oil

stock cubes
chicken or vegetable.

notes

pasta

pasta with tomato sauce

5 PEOPLE

When using dried pasta (in packets) use good quality pasta such as De Cecco, Molisana or Barilla.
Calculate about 80–100 g of pasta per person.
Cook in plenty of salted water (1½ litres of water plus 1 teaspoon of salt per 100 g of pasta).
Depending on the type of pasta, the cooking time will be between 5 to 8 minutes.
Pasta should always be 'al dente' which means 'firm to the bite', a little hard in the middle.
Pasta should be eaten immediately, unless you make a lasagne or other pasta cooked in the oven.

basic tomato sauce *for 500 g of pasta (1 packet)*

50 g unsalted butter. 2–3 tablespoons virgin olive oil.	• Melt in a saucepan.
1–2 cloves garlic, crushed. 1 red onion, finely sliced.	• Cook these in the butter and oil, until the onion goes transparent. Be careful not to burn the garlic.
5 fresh sage leaves. 1 fresh bay leaf.	• Add the herbs to the onions and cook for a few minutes.
1 tin tomato concentrate (140 g).	• Add to the above ingredients and let it cook for about 5 minutes. It will become a nice dark red.
1 tin peeled tomatoes (400 g).	• Mix well.
1 stock cube.	• Add it to the tomatoes. This will give the sauce a much stronger and richer flavour. • Cover the pan with a lid and let it simmer over low heat for about 20 minutes, stirring frequently.
5–6 fresh basil leaves, sliced.	• Add them at the end. Now remove the bay leaf and throw it away. Taste for salt and pepper.

kitchen implements

pasta with tomato sauce

VARIATIONS To basic tomato sauce add:

1 1 tin of tuna, drained of its oil and 5 anchovies. Cook for another 10 minutes. Use fusilli or conchiglie pasta.
2 300 ml cream (this sauce is called 'Mamma Rosa'). Use penne or fusilli pasta.
3 100 g pitted olives roughly chopped, 1 chilli, 6 anchovy fillets also chopped (this is called 'Puttanesca'). Use linguine or tagliatelle pasta.

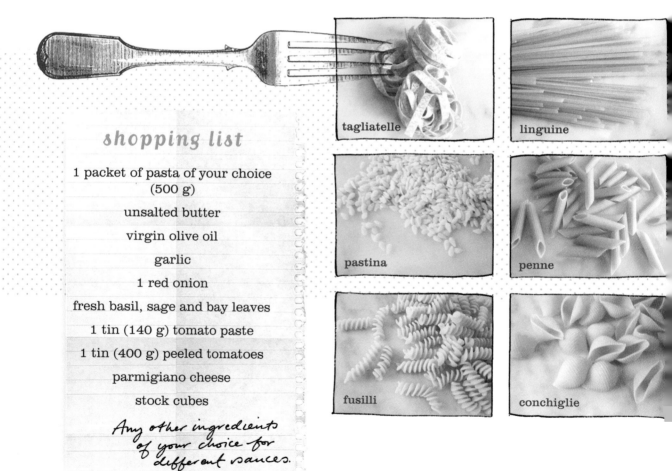

shopping list

1 packet of pasta of your choice (500 g)

unsalted butter

virgin olive oil

garlic

1 red onion

fresh basil, sage and bay leaves

1 tin (140 g) tomato paste

1 tin (400 g) peeled tomatoes

parmigiano cheese

stock cubes

Any other ingredients of your choice for different sauces.

tagliatelle

linguine

pastina

penne

fusilli

conchiglie

notes

rice

risotto

6 PEOPLE

Use 2 handfuls of rice per person plus 2 for the pot. But I think it is a good idea to make more risotto than you need as it is delicious heated up the next day. If you have fresh chicken stock, this is the time to use it; if not, use a very good quality stock cube, either chicken or vegetable.

2 litres fresh chicken stock or 2 litres water plus 4–5 stock cubes.	• Boil in a saucepan. • The stock has to be strong in flavour as it gives the risotto its flavour.
1 large onion, finely chopped. 80 g unsalted butter. 2–3 tablespoons virgin olive oil.	• Melt the butter and oil in a second large saucepan and add the onions. • Let them cook gently until they become transparent, about 5 minutes.
500 g arborio or carnaroli rice.	• Add these to the onion mixture. Turn the heat up a little higher, mix well with a wooden spoon and cook for a few more minutes.
1 glass dry white wine.	• Pour wine into the pan, stir vigorously until it has evaporated.
half the boiling stock.	• Now add half the boiling stock to the rice. Stir the risotto constantly; the more stock you can incorporate into the rice, the tastier the risotto. As the rice absorbs the stock, add more stock until it has all been used up. If the risotto seems too dry, add a little hot water (if you have run out of stock). The cooking time will be about 15–18 minutes. Risotto should still be 'al dente' (firm to the bite). Take the saucepan off the heat.
50 g unsalted butter.	• Now add the butter.
100 g freshly grated parmigiano. salt and pepper to taste.	• Mix it all well into the risotto and serve immediately. Risotto does NOT wait!

kitchen implements

risotto al salto

THIS IS A GREAT WAY TO USE YOUR LEFTOVER RISOTTO

- In a non-stick frying pan, melt 50 g unsalted butter.
- Add the leftover risotto and spread it out flat.
- Put the cooktop heat on low.
- If you have a lid, put a lid over the risotto and let it cook very gently for about 10 minutes.
- Remove the lid and with a wooden spoon press down on the risotto making it all even and flat.
- Turn up the heat a little and let it cook uncovered for another 5 minutes.
- Turn the risotto upside down by covering the frying pan with a large serving plate and flipping it over. Be careful you do not burn yourself as the pan is very hot. Use a thick tea towel.
- You should have a beautiful golden brown crust on your risotto.

risotto

VARIATIONS

1 Into the stock, add 1 packet frozen chopped spinach (it will thaw when the stock boils). You will have a green risotto.

2 Halfway through cooking the risotto, add 6–8 slices of cooked ham that you have diced, and a packet of fresh or frozen peas. This risotto is called 'Risi e Bisi'.

3 Cut fresh asparagus into 2 cm pieces. Reserve the tips and add the stalks once you have added the stock to the risotto. In the last 5 minutes of cooking, add the asparagus tips.

4 If you can find fresh zucchini with the flowers attached, cut the zucchini into little rondels and add them to the rice before you add the wine. Roughly cut the zucchini flowers and add them in the last 5 minutes of cooking the risotto.

shopping list

1 packet arborio or carnaroli rice (500 g)

chicken or vegetable stock cubes

1 large red onion
a yellow one will also do.

unsalted butter

virgin olive oil

dry white wine

parmigiano cheese

any other vegetables to do a variation to the classic risotto.

notes

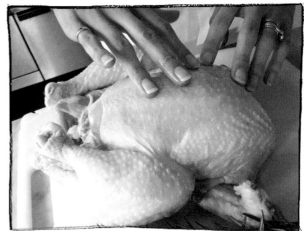

chicken

whole chicken roasted in its juices

4 PEOPLE

Buy an organic chicken. They are more expensive, but well worth it and healthier!

	• Preheat the oven to 220°C.
1 large organic chicken.	• Wash it under cold running water inside and out, then dry it well with kitchen paper towels inside and out.
2 tablespoons virgin olive oil. 2 tablespoons salt.	• Rub the chicken all over with the oil and then do the same with the salt.
6 fresh sprigs of rosemary. 1 large red onion quartered.	• Put one rosemary sprig and one quarter of the onion into the cavity of the chicken (between the legs).
1 large oven bag. 1 teaspoon flour.	• Put the flour into the oven bag and shake the bag well. Put 2 sprigs of rosemary and 2 onion quarters into the bottom of the bag. • Now gently slide the chicken into the bag and place it on top of the onion and rosemary. Put the last of the rosemary and onion between the chicken's thighs. • Tie the oven bag together with a piece of string. • Cut 2 little holes on the top side of the bag, so that the bag does not explode when cooking.
	• Cook for 1–1½ hours, depending on the size of the bird. Chicken should always be well cooked, never pink. To make sure it is cooked, push a skewer into the thickest part of the bird (the breast). If the juices run clear, it is done. If they run pink or bloody, cook a little longer.

kitchen implements

+ oven bag

whole chicken roasted in its juices

VARIATIONS

1 To make it a full meal, put a few potatoes into the bag with the chicken.

2 Or, you can fill a large saucepan with water and add:
- the chicken
- 3 celery sticks cut into large chunks
- 2 carrots, cut into chunks
- 1 large onion cut in half
- bunch of Italian parsley
- salt to taste.

Put the lid on the saucepan and boil for about 1½–2 hours over a gentle heat. This is the best meal when you're feeling a bit under the weather!

3 To make fresh chicken stock, keep all the bones of your roast chicken. Put them in a large saucepan and cover with cold water; add 1 onion, 3 celery sticks, 3 carrots and some bay leaves. Cover and let it gently boil for up to 2 hours. Let it cool a bit, then strain it through a colander. You can keep the broth in the fridge for up to 4 days, or put it in an empty ice-cream container and freeze it (it will keep up to 3 months).

shopping list

1 organic chicken

the size depends on how many people you have to feed, but remember, cold chicken is delicious, in sandwiches etc.

1–2 red onions

fresh rosemary

virgin olive oil

salt

large oven bag

they usually come in packs of four.

notes

"Taste that Chicken!"

beef

roasted beef with spicy sauce

6 PEOPLE

The best but most expensive cut is the eye fillet. It is incredibly tender. You can use scotch fillet
if you like. Scotch has a bit of fat through the meat – it is also very tasty but not as tender.

- Preheat the oven to 200°C.

MAKE A MARINADE WITH:
2 cloves garlic, crushed.
juice of 1 lemon.
½ cup sweet soy.
¼ cup virgin olive oil.
1 chilli chopped (*optional*).

1 kg fillet of beef or
  scotch fillet. *Get your*
  butcher to tie the fillet.

- Mix all these ingredients in a roasting pan.
- Put the meat into the marinade and roll it around to
  cover it well all over. Let it stand for about 30 minutes.
- If you have a cast iron grill, let it get very hot by putting
  it on top of your cooktop. Otherwise, put one tablespoon of
  olive oil into a frying pan, let it get hot, then quickly sear
  the meat on all sides so that it becomes brown all over.
- Put the meat back into the marinade in the roasting tin
  and cook it in the preheated oven for:
  15 minutes for rare.
  20 minutes for medium.
  25 minutes for well-done.
- Take the meat out of the oven and let it stand for about
  5–10 minutes before cutting it. This will make the cutting
  easier and also the juices will stay in the meat. Remove
  the string.
- The other way to see if the meat is done is to press it with
  your finger, then press the inside of the base of your thumb.
  If it feels soft like that, the meat is rare. The softer the meat
  feels, the rarer it is.
- This meat is also delicious eaten cold.

kitchen implements

roasted beef with spicy sauce

shopping list

1 kg eye fillet or scotch fillet
get your butcher to tie the eye fillet for you.

garlic

1 lemon

1 chilli

sweet soy sauce
I like to use the Indonesian ABC brand with the red label.

virgin olive oil

crushing garlic

notes

fish

whole baked fish

2 PEOPLE

Buy a whole fish: snapper, brim, perch, kingfish, or salmon. You will know if the fish is fresh because the eye will be like a 'glass' eye – clear, shiny and not sunken in.
A fish of about 30 cm long will feed 2 people.
Get the fishmonger to scale and gut the fish for you.

	• Preheat the oven to 200°C.
	• Wash the fish under cold running water, inside and out. • Now dry it well with paper towels, inside and out. • With a sharp knife, make two parallel incisions on each side of the fish.
2 tablespoons virgin olive oil.	• Rub the fish all over with the oil.
2 teaspoons salt.	• Rub the fish inside and out with the salt.
fresh thyme, oregano or bay leaves *(depending on what herbs you like).*	• Put some of the herbs into the incisions and into the stomach of the fish.
	• Rub a little extra oil into a roasting tin, put the fish on it and bake in the preheated oven for about 15–20 minutes, depending on the size of your fish. It is better to undercook fish slightly than overcook it or it will become too dry.
	• You can tell if a fish is cooked by inserting a knife into the incisions – the knife will slide easily all the way to the bone.

kitchen implements

whole baked fish

SECOND TO NONE

VARIATIONS

1 Prepare the fish as per the whole baked fish recipe.
   - Now wrap the fish in a piece of greaseproof paper, like a parcel.
   - Tie the parcel together with string, so that it will hold together.
   - Bake in the oven for about 20 minutes, again depending on the size of the fish. This method is called 'al cartoccio'.

2 By using different herbs, your fish will taste different every time. Put some fresh lemongrass and ginger pieces into the fish's stomach and incisions and bake it 'al cartoccio' as above.

3 Put the cleaned fish into a roasting tin. In the fish's incisions and stomach put some fresh bay leaves. Pour 1 glass of dry white wine over the fish, then add a handful of pitted olives of your choice, 2–3 diced fresh tomatoes, salt and pepper, and bake in the preheated oven for about 20 minutes, depending on the size of your fish. This is called 'Pesce in Carpione'.

LE BON PÊCHEUR
MARQUE DEPOSÉE

shopping list

1 whole fresh fish of your choice

virgin olive oil

fresh herbs of your choice

salt

notes

GUARANTEED FINEST QUALITY

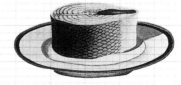

vegetables

roasted mixed vegetables

4 PEOPLE

You can use any vegetables that you like and that are in season.
The easiest way to cook them is in the oven.
In AUTUMN and WINTER, you can use for instance: potatoes, pumpkin, parsnips, red onions, sweet
potatoes, beetroots.

Per person, you calculate (depending on appetite): 1 medium potato. 1 piece pumpkin. parsnips. ½ sweet potato. 1 medium beetroot. 1 onion. *You can really use your imagination – there are no rules.*	• Preheat the oven to 200°C. • Peel all the vegetables, halve or quarter them to roughly the same size. This makes the cooking time easier to judge. • Take a large roasting tin; pour 2 tablespoons of virgin olive oil into the tin. • Put all vegetables in the tin and shake them around, so they are well coated with the oil. Try not to overcrowd the tin. If you have too many vegetables, use 2 roasting tins.
fresh rosemary, sage or bay leaf.	• Add a few sprigs of fresh rosemary, sage or bay leaf.
	• Now put the roasting tin into the preheated oven for about 30 minutes. The time depends a bit on the sizes of the vegetables. They should be golden and a little crisp. From time to time during the cooking process, shake the roasting tin in order to loosen the vegetables from the bottom.
salt to taste.	• Take them out of the oven and sprinkle the vegetables with salt.

kitchen implements

roasted mixed vegetables

VARIATIONS In **SPRING** and **SUMMER** you could use:

fresh beans, broccolini (baby broccoli), asparagus, English spinach.
The way to prepare these vegetables is to bring some water to the boil in
a medium saucepan; add 2 teaspoons of salt, then the vegetables and cook
for 2–3 minutes only. They should still be crunchy. Drain and drizzle with
some virgin olive oil and a little salt. You do not even have to cook the
leaf spinach – just toss it in with the hot vegetables on a serving plate
and that will be sufficient.

shopping list

this is for four people.

4 medium potatoes

butternut pumpkin

3 parsnips

1 long sweet potato

*I love the white variety
as they taste a little like
chestnuts but the orange
ones are fine.*

3–4 medium beetroots

4 medium red onions

fresh sage, rosemary
or bay leaves

virgin olive oil

salt

FOR THE GREEN VEGETABLES
also for four people.

200 g baby French beans

2 bunches of asparagus

200 g broccolini

150 g English spinach

virgin olive oil

salt

notes

VEGETABLES

green salad

mixed salad with a classic dressing

4 PEOPLE

Choose any green salad such as mignonette lettuce, baby
English spinach,
rocket, iceberg.

- You can choose any combination of lettuces or you can buy an already mixed salad at your greengrocer or supermarket.
- Wash the leaves under running cold water to remove any sand or dirt. Discard any yellow or wilted leaves. Put the washed leaves in a colander and shake off any excess water.
- Put them in to a serving bowl. If you are not eating the salad immediately put it in the fridge. It will stay crisp.

---

juice of 1 lemon.
1 teaspoon salt.
1 teaspoon French mustard.
½ cup virgin olive oil.

- Now prepare the dressing. Put all the dressing ingredients into a jar with a screw-top lid. Close it well and shake it vigorously. The dressing will become pale yellow and smooth.
- Just before serving the salad, pour the dressing over it. Always do this at the last minute, or the salad will become limp and discolour.

- This salad dressing will keep for at least one week in the fridge.

kitchen implements

mixed salad with a classic dressing

rocket

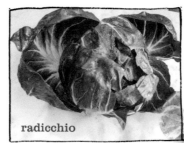

radicchio

mignonette

iceberg

shopping list

lettuces
of your choice

1 lemon

virgin olive oil

salt

French mustard

notes

sorbet

raspberry sorbet and ice-cream

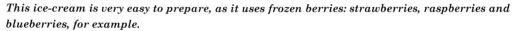

6 PEOPLE

This ice-cream is very easy to prepare, as it uses frozen berries: strawberries, raspberries and blueberries, for example.
You will see that by leaving the fruits frozen, you will create instant ice-creams and sorbets.
You do not need an ice-cream machine!

raspberry sorbet

600 g frozen raspberries.
juice of 1 lemon.
50 g caster sugar.

- Put all the ingredients into a bowl (the berries should still be frozen) and with your kitchen wiz, blend them until the mass becomes smooth and silky.
- The sorbet should be quite tart in taste. If you prefer it sweeter, just add a little more sugar.

raspberry ice-cream

600 g frozen raspberries.
50 g caster sugar.
300 ml full cream.

- Put all the ingredients into a bowl and with your kitchen wiz, blend until you will get a smooth ice-cream.

kitchen implements

raspberry sorbet and ice-cream

shopping list

600 g frozen berries
of your choice

1 lemon

caster sugar

300 ml thick cream

notes

pasta

pepper

soy sauce

virgin olive oil

vinegar

bread

(keep some in the freezer)

butter

anchovies

salt

tinned tuna

tomato concentrate

eggs

stock cubes

flour

sugar

rice

coffee or tea

oven bags

pelati

(tinned tomatoes)

top 10 *mysteries of the kitchen*

Every oven is different. Some have symbols; others have words and numbers.

LOW OVEN	120°–150°C
MEDIUM OVEN	180°–200°C
HIGH OVEN	220°–240°C
GRILL	Cooks only the top of the food. Ideal for chops, steak, cheese on toast.
NORMAL OVEN	Heat is on the top and bottom. Ideal for roasts, baked pastas, cakes, fish, vegetables etc.
FAN-FORCED OVENS	Heat is on the top and bottom as per a normal oven, but because of the fan the heat is more evenly distributed. Ideal for cakes and biscuits.

When in a recipe it says 'preheat the oven' you should turn the oven on about 30 minutes before you start to cook.

to crush

to shave

to slice

to peel

to chop

to dice

top 10 *tips*

keep it clean!

Before cooking, always wash your hands!

Make sure that the surface you are going to prepare the food on is clean.

When you have finished with an implement, wash it as you go along, otherwise you will be left with a mountain of dishes.

Soak the pots and pans in hot water after you have finished using them. Do not leave the washing up until the next day, or it will be hard work!

If the fridge smells, wash it out with some white vinegar and water.

Always wrap your food in cling wrap when storing in the fridge.

eggs

Always choose organic eggs. They taste so much better, are better for you and the yolks are a wonderful dark yellow.

When you boil an egg, prick the round side of the egg with a pin before you put it in boiling water. This will prevent the egg from cracking. Every egg has a little pocket of air; by pricking the egg, the air can escape and the shell will not crack.

SOFT-BOILED EGGS: Taken from the fridge, boil for 4 minutes. At room temperature, boil for 3 minutes.

MEDIUM-BOILED EGGS: Taken from the fridge, boil for 5 minutes. At room temperature, boil for 4 minutes.

HARD-BOILED EGGS: Taken from the fridge, boil for 8 minutes. At room temperature, boil for 7 minutes.

Hard-boiled eggs can be stored in the fridge for up to 4 days.

To know if an egg is still fresh, fill a jug with cold water and gently lower the egg into the water. If the egg sinks, it is fresh; if it tilts slightly, it is still OK; but if it floats fully to a vertical position, throw it out!

To know if an egg you've kept in the fridge is cooked or raw, spin the egg on the table. If it spins fast, it is cooked; if not, it is raw.

If the eggs stick to the carton, wet the carton and you will be able to remove them.

If the lid does not open from a jar, tap the lid with a hard object all around. This will break the seal, some air will get into the jar and you will be able to open it.

In order not to cry when peeling onions, wet the chopping board and your hand before chopping them.

salt

When do you add the salt?
- In soups and sauces, add it at the beginning.
- For vegetables, salt the water at the beginning.
- For meats, salt them when you have finished cooking them.

Always try the food before adding salt. You can always add more, but you can't take it away.

If your soup is too salty, add cream, water or milk.

the freezer

You can freeze all sort of things. Bread is great to freeze. Take it out of the freezer and put the frozen loaf in a warm oven. It will become crunchy. For sliced bread, put the slices straight from freezer to toaster.

Soups and sauces freeze really well. Remember to always label each dish.

Once you have frozen something you CANNOT re-freeze it again!

to revive things

If you have a loaf of bread that has become stale, wet it with a little water using your hands then put it in a preheated oven (180°C) for about 15 minutes and it will become crunchy again.

To keep fresh herbs and salad crisp, wet a paper bag, add the herbs and salad and put them in your fridge drawer.

If you peel potatoes and are not cooking them straight away, put them in a bowl of cold water (otherwise they will become brown). By putting them in the fridge with a few drops of lemon juice, they will keep for up to 3 days.

This edition published in 2008 by
Hardie Grant Books
85 High Street
Prahran, Victoria 3181, Australia
www.hardiegrant.com.au

First published in 2008 by
Manuela Food and Travel
12 Ginahgulla Road
Bellevue Hill NSW 2023, Australia
www.manuelafoodandtravel.com

Cataloguing-in-Publication data is available
from the National Library of Australia.

ISBN 978 1 74066 676 3

Design by Pfisterer+Freeman

Printed and bound in China by C&C Offset Printing

10 9 8 7 6 5 4 3 2 1